A
SMALL
BOOK

A Small Book © 2024 B Nester

All Rights Reserved. No part of this book may be reproduced in any form or by any electronic or mechanical means including information storage and retrieval systems, without permission in writing from the author. The only exception is by a reviewer, who may quote short excerpts in a review.

This book is a work of non-fiction. Every effort has been made to trace or contact all copyright holders. The publishers will be pleased to make good any omissions or rectify any mistakes brought to their attention at the earliest opportunity.

Printed in Australia

Cover and internal design by Shawline Publishing Group Pty Ltd

First printing: March 2024

Shawline Publishing Group Pty Ltd

www.shawlinepublishing.com.au

Paperback ISBN 978-1-9231-0171-5

eBook ISBN 978-1-9231-0172-2

Distributed by Shawline Distribution and Lightning Source Global

Shawline Publishing Group acknowledges the traditional owners of the land and pays respects to the Elders, past, present and future.

 A catalogue record for this work is available from the National Library of Australia

A
SMALL
BOOK

*Remembering important truths
in a complicated world*

A

SMALL

BOOK

Remember the important truths
in a complicated world

CONTENTS

1. A Small Book	1
2. A Small Line	7
3. A Small Explanation	11
4. A Small Rule	21
5. A Small Lie	25
6. A Small Word	29
7. The Bad News	35
8. The Good News	43
9. The Hard News	47
10. Time	59
11. Keeping it Real	65
12. Who Am I to Direct this Small Book to You?	73
13 One Small Thing	77
14. The Final Page	81

Chapter 1

A Small Book

This book is dedicated to you.
Written for you.
With you specifically in mind.

I have been fortunate to spend much of my life learning about how people get through their days. This has helped me understand what makes some journey's just a little easier; a little brighter.

If you find yourself trapped in a world of discontent, sadness, loneliness, anger, loss, confusion, frustration, lack of motivation, financial strain, ill health, lacking hope or just plain lost, the message in this small book may be exactly what you've been looking for.

If by chance fate has put this small book into your hands and you are now taking the journey to live the simple answer in its pages, it is my hope you will find guidance and relief from whatever darkness shadows your way, today and for many days to come.

These brief words may be used time and time again, in all manner of circumstance. Irrespective of who you are but mostly... because of it!

Notice your hands as they hold these pages. Do they feel warm, or are they cold? Are your eyes heavy or comfortable? Notice your shoulders. Are they tight and high or low and at ease? This is life happening to you. Right now.

You are the most important part of this moment, this reality.

My own reality finds me picking through a million words and the experiences of many to reach you through the print on this page. To help you hear one line. It is a line heard far too seldomly for the wisdom and chance for change it holds.

But this book is not just to be read. You play a bigger part in its existence than merely as its reader. Whether you choose to do nothing with the information I am sharing with you, or whether you do much, you have become part of its story from the moment you picked it up.

There is a personal price to pay for reading the words being shared within this cover, for letting their patterns take shape in your mind. The price is this: You cannot unknow them. While these pages cannot give you your answers, it can give you something much more timeless and powerful.

Questions and answers come and go. With every moment we change and confuse them with our clever words, excuses, perceptions, assumptions and feelings. I want to offer you something far stronger.

I offer you ownership of this life, of your life.

A wise old friend once said to me, 'I can tell you, but know this, with all knowledge comes responsibility.'

If you are ready to take on that responsibility in return for the freedom wisdom brings…

Welcome, brave warrior… Read on.

Chapter 2

A Small Line

A Small Book

YOU HAVE A CHOICE.

Chapter 3

A Small Explanation

That's it!?

Seems ridiculous, doesn't it?

Four words. Too simple to take seriously. But, as many know, while simple may be best, it is rarely easy. Yet, you're still here with me, so... let me explain.

Apart from when life leaves you, there is never a circumstance where you do not have the power of choice. No matter how shitty, desperate, lonely, or hard it may seem. Even in the cruellest of situations, where your freedom has been stolen, your health steals your ability to live with dignity or hope or even when the greatest of all wrongs occurs and the use of your words, beliefs or body are taken from you, **<u>NO ONE</u>** can take your ability to choose.

This four-word statement applies to everyone from the homeless to the elite. Every successful person, from the world of business to the realms of religion, politics, learning, entertainment or sport have been where you are RIGHT NOW. And they have made choice after choice after choice to get themselves to where they are RIGHT NOW.

By this I mean they have faced moments of hardship, trials, sadness, worthlessness, hopelessness and doubt. They have made choice, after choice, after choice to get to the level of success where they shine brightest and then they've kept making choices that influence whether they shine even brighter, stay where they are or shine a little less. Provided you hurt no one else, there are no bad choices.

<u>'You're gonna be dead.'</u>

My daughters are very familiar with this phrase. In the past I have even threatened to have it tattooed on some inconspicuous part of their body so that when I can no longer remind them, they will still remember. It is the truest, most unchangeable, unarguable fact for every single one of us. It is the only absolute truth in every single person's life on this planet. It is why everything matters and yet nothing matters. How you choose to use that knowledge is unique to every individual. In light of the truth this statement brings, wouldn't you rather spend your days alive making choices that make you – and in turn others – feel better while you have the opportunity?

You have a choice. Is knowing that going to turn you into Nelson Mandela, Gina Rinehart, Richard Branson, Dylon Alcott, Ash Barty, Usain Bolt, Margot Robbie, The Rock, Anh Do, Mother Teresa or the Dalai Lama? Not without making informed choices and definitely not without the action that follows your choices. Repeatedly.

Another bonus using this line in your life can bring is this: THE CHOICES ARE ALL YOURS! Those choices can be as small as your response to any given moment all the way through to the most complex of choices.

DON'T UNDERESTIMATE THE POWER OF CHOICE. THE CHOICE OF HOW YOU RESPOND TO ANYTHING IS WITHOUT DOUBT THE BIGGEST GAME CHANGER OF YOUR EXISTENCE.

This applies whether your choice is to get out of bed, to forgive yourself or forgive someone else, exercise, eat better, decide what to wear, let go, or try something new.

Whether it is to smile, help someone feel good, work less, move more, choose who to surround yourself with or get help to feel better, provided you follow the Golden Rule of never hurting yourself or others, you <u>CAN</u> move on.

Even if choosing to move on for you means choosing to stay right where you are! The power of this line is such that if you make and act on your choice and it turns out to be a bad one (and here comes the magic... prepare yourself... your mind is about to be blown), you can then choose to make a better, more informed choice!

This means **YOU CAN NOT FAIL** when making a choice.

Making an informed choice allows you to be who YOU want to be in the world. There is no wrong answer because:

a) You can learn from a bad choice that didn't work for you and evolve to make a different choice, and

b) The world will carry on irrespective of, and also because of, which choices you make!

We live in a world of privilege today. Never in the history of humanity has there been more access to self-learning, phone help, counselling, coaching, spiritual guidance, support, philosophy, medicine, professionals, volunteer organisations, government organisations, libraries, internet and education. The vast majority of which (in our lucky country of Australia especially) can be free to a large degree.

The Universal Declaration of Human Rights exists to remind every human on this planet that 'all human beings are born free and equal in dignity and rights'. That 'everyone has the right to life, liberty and the security of person'. And that includes **YOU**.

If you aren't living a life that emulates these rights it may be simply that you haven't been given permission or knowledge to chase life or freedom as an individual. Most successful people either give themselves this permission or it is given to them by a parent as a child, or perhaps by a teacher, partner, coach or friend. Sometimes people may be given this permission by a mentor or simply from a character in a book or TV show that they admire. If you haven't been given it before, this small book exists to give it to you now.

Permission to become YOUR BEST SELF. The best version of you.

Another reason you may not be living by these rights might be because at some point in your life so far, some, or even many, of your choices were taken from you by force, coercion or manipulation. There is so much wrongness in this that I don't have strong enough words to convey my thoughts. I can, however, offer you this truth. You are strong and have proven that by making it through to THIS exact moment.

Simply the fact you are holding this book, looking for

more ways to make things in your world better is proof of this.

It's okay to feel angry, to feel cheated, to feel sad. It is equally okay to feel okay, to achieve, to be more than you were yesterday and more than you are today.

It is also okay to stay exactly as you are. It is okay to feel any way you choose to. We know as humans we all end up in the same place. Isn't it a smarter choice to choose to feel better along the way!

The beauty of this small line is that it can be used a million times a day in a million different ways. You are never stuck. There is always a choice, and if your choice turns out to be wrong, then you can make a BETTER one. I'm not being a smartass when I say that. Seriously think about it. This is pure unadulterated magic.

The alchemy of life where instead of turning metal to gold you are turning all the things you could possibly be into your reality.

Whether your choice is to act alone, educate yourself to find a better way, get support, support someone else, eat better, change careers, accept what you cannot change, end a toxic relationship, rest, stop taking drugs/alcohol, end self-criticism, stop procrastinating, believe in yourself, work harder, travel, be kind to yourself or someone else, learn to say no or any one of thousands of other options, or even to simply stay exactly as you are, IT'S YOUR CHOICE!

Provided you follow the Golden Rule…

Chapter 4

A Small Rule

Never make choices that hurt yourself or someone else.

This rule is essential to protect yourself as much as everyone else. Why would I go to the trouble of sharing a book about the fact you have choices if you are going to make ones that hurt yourself or someone else? How do you know if your choices are right?

If you lay your head down at the end of the day and feel peace and satisfaction with who your choices have shaped you to become and you've hurt no one in acting on them, you can know you're doing something right.

When you are tough enough to pick the choices that make you uncomfortable enough to grow, it becomes impossible not to follow this rule.

In making choices that allow you to become your best, you learn tolerance and respect for everyone else's choices. You start to recognise how tough some choices can be to make and act on, which can give you more respect for other people's stories.

The Latin phrase 'Primum non nocere' from the Hippocratic Oath means '<u>First, do no harm</u>'. It is the rule sworn to and followed by professionals of healing the world over.

It is as true for us as we heal ourselves.

While it is true that you have a choice, even if that choice is simply how you choose to respond to every moment in your life, so too is it true that EVERY person that draws breath or has a heart that beats has a right to their own safety, happiness and betterment.

THIS INCLUDES YOU!

The Golden Rule exists to protect these… **YOUR** inalienable rights.

Chapter 5

A Small Lie

'Do this and life will be easier.'

This, to some degree, is a lie. Books have been written in a million different ways to advise people on methods to make their lives easier.

THIS IS NOT ONE OF THOSE BOOKS.

This book is to tell you that life will always throw curve balls at you.

It won't stop the tears or the hard times.

You've been through enough and are smart enough to know life doesn't work that way. This is also why it takes a brave warrior to read this book.

Because making ACTIVE choices (that's right… choices followed by action), being honest with your excuses, wants and needs, and being strong enough to **own** and **act** your choices and responses *is hard…* REALLY hard.

Luckily for you, you are part of the animal species known as Homosapien and as such, you are not only entitled, but practically guaranteed, to muck up at some point. After all, we really are only human. At this point I feel like you know where I'm headed next…

Mistakes are an unavoidable part of the human condition. Sometimes they are brilliant, sometimes a disaster. Either way, how you respond, and what your next move is (you guessed it…) YOUR CHOICE.

In some ways life can be *too* easy today. We look for 'badness' in our lives and amplify it just to feel worthy of people's interest. It's almost embarrassing to say we are not run off our feet, unhappy, feeling like crap, raging against the establishment, underpaid, heartbroken, or just plain tired, particularly here in Australia. It's somehow become embarrassing to do well or feel good.

Complaining or struggling has become a way to give us common ground to connect with each other and fight a common foe. It makes us comrades, but also… it stops us feeling good about things working out.

This stuff is not rocket science, it's logical common sense. But that doesn't make it any easier. In fact, it's enough to throw you into a spiral of saying, 'Well, if it's so easy, why aren't I already doing it!? On top of everything else that's happened in my world, you are going to make me feel like I am failing at something as simple as making good choices too?' The answer is just as simple.

You're *not* failing.

Up to this point in your existence, maybe no one let you in on this massive truth. Or maybe you have just had so much crap dumped on you so repeatedly, that your memory of this truth was smothered, making it a struggle to simply keep going, let alone remember. Yet still, you have battled through.

Now you know the unarguable truth of this small book, you can use your struggles, both past and present.

Your struggle exists as a sign that begs you to choose to make different choices.

In the dance of life, use the sticks that beat the drum to find a new beat, not to beat yourself.

Anger, fear and sometimes even sadness can channel choices that reflect their darkness.

Know that you can also choose to use the same energy that negativity generates, to be everything it is not.

Chapter 6

A Small Word

Responsibility.

There was a time this word sent chills through me. I would go to great extremes to avoid anything that even remotely involved responsibility. That changed when I learnt how to understand it as a way to be free, rather than a punishment full of burden and restraint.

This word isn't heavy with limitation, work and obligation. It is simply a meshing of two words that remind us we have the ability to respond – a response ability. The ability to **choose how** we respond is the key.

For example, I didn't have to write this book.

I chose to. It is my response to my life so far.

You didn't have to pick it up and read it.

You chose to. It is your response to this moment in *your* life.

You're not obligated one way or another to like it, agree with it or disagree with it. The response is solely your own choice.

Just like you, I am living my own choices. And, just as you sometimes may be, I too am riddled with feelings of unworthiness, discontent, anger, fear and sadness. My experiences of hurt, mistakes, let downs, mistreatment, lack of education, guidance and opportunity create doubt within me.

Doubt that is aiming to protect me from failing again, to protect me from the discomfort that trying something different brings. It is trying to protect me from being judged or criticised, to protect me from other people's choices.

Everyday challenges in the form of money troubles, illness, other people, work and time restraints are all things seemingly out of my control. They all give the illusion of holding me back.

But that is all it is.

An illusion.

Life's challenges invite opportunities to invent excuses disguised as reasons about not choosing a different way to approach my world. They bring feelings… deep feelings that make it okay and even necessary to say, 'I can't, too hard, I don't have enough money/time/ability'. But this is all in an effort to protect myself.

You can only break through this default setting by saying, 'Thanks for protecting me brain, I'll keep it all in mind. But right now I am making the choice to try. I am choosing to change my responses and actions to find better feelings, a better me, a better life'.

If that turns out wrong, I'll choose another way.

I'll choose to say, 'Nice work for giving it a crack, me!' and move on to another day and another choice.

It's okay to wallow in your circumstances but know it is also your choice to.

Sometimes it's not only okay to roll around in your sadness and dissatisfaction, it is necessary.

How else will you know what you want or don't want?

How else will you know what you will fight for or accept?

How else can we let it go if we don't feel it first?

How long we stay trapped in those feelings once they have served their purpose however, **IS A CHOICE**. The choice of how you respond to the world, people and events is yours and no one else's.

Own it.

You most often get from life what you put your focus on.

It doesn't matter if you are not a doctor, philosopher or scientist. It doesn't matter if you never went to school at all. It doesn't matter your financial status or level of success or even your age.

You don't need money or a degree to know whether something you are doing in your life is working for you or not. In fact, ***only you*** can know that. Just like no one but you can know what you're prepared to do to accept it or change it.

For all anyone else knows, maybe complaining or being unhappy about your situation is something that you really prefer. Maybe it suits you to go over and over the same situations you find yourself in. Maybe that choice is what floats your boat. And if it does and it doesn't hurt anyone else, then all the very best to you.

Perhaps you will get to the end of this small book, consider your own good self and say, 'Nope, I don't feel I need to change a thing'. To which I say to you, 'That's great! Perfect!' Perhaps you are choosing to accept where you are today and own the choices that brought you here and are happy to keep on perfectly well as you are.

That's as true a choice as any change you might make. The point is that **YOU** are choosing that response.

YOU are the dictator of your destiny and the captain of your own boat and for that I have only admiration.

That is the whole point of this small book – to own where you are in your life and be accountable for your ability to respond to that moment.

Whether you do or whether you don't, please don't just sit on the fence, for everything you do or don't has a consequence.

Whether you choose to change your underwear or the world… the choices are yours! You make them every second of your day.

Own them.

We live in a world of choices, all from our own making.

<u>OWN THAT WORLD. IT IS YOURS.</u>

Chapter 7

The Bad News

Making choices is not an easy thing to do because it often involves being honest with yourself about these very difficult things:

- **Firstly**, being accountable for your own part in any circumstance in your world.
- **Secondly**, being *honest* enough with yourself about whether you care enough to make a different choice.
- **Finally**, being strong enough to act on a choice using any and all means possible.

Bad partners and bullies rely on us choosing to feel worthless, subservient, controlled and scared.

Statespeople in every democracy around the world rely on your choices every day. As do the media, big corporations, entertainment, technology, grocery stores, clothing retailers and restaurants. The very world economy rests on your choices.

Wise men from Socrates to Nietzsche have advised us over and again about the importance of our choices regarding response and belief. Either way, no matter what is done to us or happens around us, the choice of how we respond and act is our own. It sounds so stupidly simple, but it is what we find at every crossroads on our way forward through life.

We are all guilty of wrapping ourselves protectively in excuses, sadness, fear or helplessness to cope with our life situation at some point. Even though all this does is sink us even further into the deep darkness of suffering.

'What a tangled web we weave. When first we practise to deceive!' wrote Sir Walter Scott. He wasn't joking!

The lies we tell those around us, but most especially ourselves, entangle us in a world of confusion and fear. They make an already complicated life messier and stop broken hearts mending. They keep the strongest among us weak and warriors become lambs.

Then there are also the lies and perceptions of everybody else.

The promises and beliefs of media, politicians, religion, money-making enterprises and sometimes even those we love are all wrapped up in someone else's ideas and experience of reality.

All of these go toward muddying up the waters of real understanding and clear choices even further. How do we navigate this web?

No one knows you better than yourself. No one else knows who you want to become or what you want to achieve but you.

So if what you have been doing is not serving you… why are you still doing it? If drinking or partying till three a.m. numbs the pain but doesn't stop it, clearly that's not working.

If the people around you only complete you when you live up to their expectations, but you feel alone in your soul when they are gone, maybe it's time to choose to find people to surround yourself with that want you to feel complete with or without their approval. Maybe it's time to choose people who want you to feel good ALL the time. If your world is a drama-fest you despise, choose to drop the thinking by filling your head and days with learning and action instead.

If the person you are pouring all your love into and living to make happy doesn't want the same happiness and love for you, **choose to know** you are just as deserving of that love, respect and care as anyone else on the planet. Keeping a toxic mindset even though you have proven to yourself over and again that it doesn't make you feel good, instead of choosing to vigilantly watch over how you think and act and do things differently is a choice, it's just not one that's going to help you.

The examples are endless. From the clothes you choose to wear and the words you choose to speak, to the job you choose to keep to pay the bills you choose to create and the way you choose to treat every person you meet through your day.

I challenge you to go forward from reading this book, knowing what you now know and tell me this book isn't about you or for you.

When every part of your life has choice strewn through it, even if at the very bare end, the choice may be as simple as the choosing how to respond to a situation with forgiveness, or acceptance and peace, or let something or someone go and move on. It could be to choose to be angry, disappointed, or sad enough to fight for a different situation. Or to choose to do nothing at all and let life's circumstances and the emotions they evoke come and go.

Don't get me wrong, sometimes stuff happens in your world that is really, really hard to bear. Stuff that breaks your heart or rips your soul to shreds.

Sometimes things will happen out of your control that bring you down so hard that just looking for choices, let alone making them, seems about as possible as waking up with the ability to speak another language fluently whilst drinking a thickshake with a swollen tongue. Sometimes your life circumstances and the choices you make in how to survive through them are the difference – quite literally – between life and death.

Let me state again: this small book isn't to say you shouldn't feel your fear, sadness and misery. In fact, it's necessary you do.

How else will you know what you want or don't want, what you will fight for or against?

How else will you know what you will discard or accept, or how to let the hard bits go if we don't feel them first? How else can we know what risks we are prepared to take or what pain we are prepared to sit with?

This book is simply to remind you, whether you sit in the revolving door of life repeating how you live day after day, dwelling on all your 'if only' moments lost, or looking at all your options and choosing a new way to be in your world, or looking at your life accepting it as it is and deciding you are perfectly happy and wish to change nothing…

THIS IS A CHOICE.

All are brave, all are strong, and all are choices.

Chapter 8

The Good News

You are already doing it!

From getting out of bed, to wiping your bum. From putting food in your mouth, pulling a blanket up when you are cold or scratching an itch, all the way through to picking up this small book and continuing to turn its pages and read its words. Going to work/school and actually trying your best or doing nothing and getting nowhere, having a relationship, relishing being single, staying in a toxic situation, stepping into the unknown, trying something new or making the same good, or bad, choices over and over, all the way through to the very things you think and say.

And hey… remember to credit yourself for all the choices that you've already made that *have* worked for you! There are always so many more of them than you realise once you learn to look for them.

You are already making choices every moment of every day. I'm not asking you to do any more than you are doing already.

My guess is you have already faced demons and toughed out bad times.

In fact, you may be doing so right now. But that just proves the point that you can do so again. The strength is already within you.

YOU HAVE.

YOU CAN.

YOU ARE.

YOU WILL AGAIN.

Life will *always* throw shit at us.

Reading this book isn't going to stop that.

Nothing stops that.

What it will do is let you see that you are already stronger and smarter and have more options than you ever knew you had.

Chapter 9

The Hard News

You can't unknow this.

This means no matter what you tell yourself from this point on, you are now, in a massive way, accountable for your own 'stuff'!

You call your shots.

You decide what to do with how you feel.

***

Life's not fair.

But the biggest unfairness is the one you create yourself by not looking at your options. By not choosing something else that is better than what you are already working with.

It's not fair that children the world over are beaten mentally and physically or mistreated in the worst ways.

It's not fair that about 2.4 billion people – or roughly one third of the world's population – people in *your* world, don't have access to a toilet just from the sheer chance of being born where they are born.

It's not fair we are all born equal but live lives of inequality.

It's not fair that we are judged or not given a chance.

It's not fair to be bullied or feel invisible.

It's not fair to be given life when physical illness robs us of living it.

It's not fair to struggle with mental health.

It's not fair to be born with learning or social disabilities.

It's not fair to have had terrible childhoods or bad partners.

It's not fair to be born into violence, war or fear.

The greatest unfairness of all, however, is knowing it could be better and doing **NOTHING.**

***

On the Hardest Choice.

If you are choosing to read this and you think choosing not to participate in life anymore makes it easier for others, somehow better or less of a burden, you need to know other people's truth on this line of thinking.

The very fact that you can only know yourself means you can never realise or understand how much hurt and negativity choosing to give up on life has on those you love and even those you don't know.

It doesn't just affect the obvious people in your world but the lives of all those who your random, offhand comment could have made a difference to.

Your one kindness, your one smile, your own specific and unique style of interacting, way of caring or seeing the world makes a difference to people you may never have more to do with than passing them by in the street. Sometimes even just allowing someone else's help, you give someone else a purpose and reason to live.

I am not suggesting the responsibility of everyone else's well-being lies with you. I am suggesting you may owe it to yourself and others to exhaust every possible avenue of help before you give up on yourself.

There are a great many of those avenues to take.

Choosing to let go of life carries such an impact on so many others. It is a choice that changes the course of lives that haven't even begun, creating tendrils of doubt into future generations.

On Illness.

The dis-ease of the mind and also the dis-ease of the body make choice critical. Rarely does anyone consciously choose to be unwell. Sadly, sickness or imbalance in the body does not discriminate. You must always remember you are not your illness. It may limit you. It may change your world inside and out, but how you choose to respond to it is up to you.

On illness owning you, it should be said that it is a wise person who informs themselves of their illness, physical or mental. Equally, one must remember that when illness is a huge part of everyday survival and limits our quality of life and functionality, it can be very easy to neglect surrounding ourselves with what we want or need in our lives, as it insidiously pushes out laughter and a sense of balance in our world.

Remember this: **you are not your illness**. You are not your disability. You are not your struggle.

Who you are is the owner of the response you choose to give that illness.

The labels of illness come with all manner of mental

and physical imbalance, disability or struggle. They are not, however, the sum total of who you are.

They are the names and words used to describe easily what your specific hardwiring is. They exist to give you and those around you a better road map of what you need to be your best self.

It's not fair to have a body/brain setup that means you need to factor in conditions like bipolar or schizophrenia, cancer, heart disease or any of the thousands of possible brain/body imbalances in your life.

You can choose to let the unfairness of having to utilise these labels rule you or see them for what they are: terminology.

These labels are what we use to define how each and every mind and body operates.

If they exist in your world, doesn't that just make it even more important that you look after yourself and use them to find the best ways to do exactly that?

That you consider your best support, best information, best treatments and best way forward?

The very existence of these labels makes it important

that you notice them and then use them to find the things that work and figure out the best way to negotiate the things that don't.

Feeling good about life and being aware of your best self is even more of a priority when you aren't operating at your best.

Your illness is already robbing you of your health, time and possibly your happiness.

Do not let it rob you further than it already has.

Learning to Allow and Accept.

(When something seems simple, it usually isn't.)

A big part not often discussed about dealing with what the world throws at us is that if we want to feel better, we need to allow it.

This means breaking the cycle of looking for worry and problems.

This means not looking for a repeat of what has happened to you before, to happen once again.

It's about learning to allow a new way of feeling.

That can't happen when you are too frightened or can't remember how to just feel okay.

Humans can get very comfortable with what they know and if that is a world of hardship then, crazy as it seems, that hardship can be easier to live with than finding out how to exist without it.

Just as you must allow the sadness, the hurt and the anger that you feel, it is equally important to allow the okay times.

A large part of this means accepting what you cannot change and focusing on what you can, because for better or worse, **we experience in our life what we choose to put our focus on.**

Your Choices Are Yours Just As Other's Choices Are Theirs

Stop wasting precious time and energy on changing other people. They are living *their* idea of life.

<u>If you are spending your time trying to change them, all you are doing is neglecting or avoiding living yours.</u>
You can only change YOUR circumstances, YOUR perception and YOUR responses.

The best bit about all this bad news is that if you ever struggled through hard times, you are already tough enough to be aware of your choices.

In choosing to act on them, you were probably often surprised at how it really wasn't the big deal you thought it was going to be **<u>after</u>** you made the choice and acted on it. It's more often the moments before the doing that frightens the crap out of us. Knowing you have the ability to respond (response ability) by being aware of and making better choices is really more like a habit than a hardship.

The action that follows choice can seem hard at first because it feels different. Different can feel uncomfortable. But this is most often a sign you are challenging or changing yourself. This is good. Without challenge there can be **no change**.

On Your Story.

We all have one. There are a million and one stories about why it's hard to make good choices. Bad childhoods, traumatic experiences, crap relationships, poverty and lack of education and support, to name just a few.

The truth is your story is a collection of your choices, be they responses to circumstances out of your control or the choices you have made and acted on so far.

Every choice you make either sinks you further into a bad story or sends you on to find a better one.

It is also true that who you are right now, in this

moment, and where your next choice takes you rests entirely with you. Irrespective of or because of that story.

If you are a human with an ability that even remotely lets you make ANY choice, then there are choices to be made.

It is up to you and no one else to choose a new story or accept the current one.

There is great power in that.

Chapter 10

Time

In Australia, most of us live to be approximately eighty years old. That's 29,300 days of life. Now minus the total time you have already lived from this. (If you want a more accurate time estimate of the days you have lived, go to: timeanddate.com days calculator.)

Factor in that if you take the first sixteen years of your life away as dependant years, minus also the fact we spend roughly a third of our lives sleeping, you are left with 42.5 years left in which you are awake in your lifetime. You have roughly about 15,330 awake days to live in a lifetime. It sounds like a lot.

But how old are you today? What if you're thirty years old already? Or forty?

If you are already fifty and sleep around seven hours a night, you have approximately 7,756 awake days left.

Now calculate and minus real time spent on meal times, waiting times, showering and toilet time... time is rapidly disappearing. You don't get that back. Not one second.

<u>Who you are is the only thing in this world you have any control over!</u>

Ask yourself: 'Is the immediate situation a problem within my control or is my choice more about how I respond to the situation?

How do I choose to respond or act to any specific situation, event, circumstance, or person, current, past, or present?

Am I prepared to stay in the situation?

Am I prepared to change it?'

Though we feel like we have forever, we are alive for a moment.

It doesn't take a near death experience to appreciate what time we have. Look at the numbers above and know the days of your life are literally disappearing even as you read these words…

We are toward the end of this small book now and your eyes quite probably have the word 'choice' imprinted on their retina from seeing the word so repeatedly.

I do not apologise.

This book is about one simple thing.

You understanding and owning your choices.

But time is running out quicker than we will ever realise and between that and our own brains protecting us so indelibly, it's too vital a truth to not repeat until its importance is understood.

I'm not telling you anything you don't already know at the core of your being with this small book.

1. You always have a choice. Even if it is limited to how you respond.

2. You know yourself best.

3. You know when you're hurting someone else.

4. You know what feels right and what feels wrong.

5. You know when you're lying to yourself (even though you may not like it).

6. We all end up in the same place at the end of our lives.

We have limited time on the planet and as humans we all want pretty much the same thing… to spend that time living as happily, as satisfied and feeling as good as we can.

Choice is a fundamental survival skill that has allowed our species to get to where we are today. That's around 200,000 years of making the most basic choice of whether to fight, freeze or run just to stay alive.

With vastly many more options to choose from today, why not use it to become the best you can be?

Choices from what you eat, how you dress, how you speak, who you surround yourself with, what you buy, what you read, what you watch, what you learn, all the way through to how you respond to what life throws at you.

Your ability to choose how you respond is the most powerful of choices.

It determines how you think, who you are and who you become. It often dictates what happens next in your world or which direction your path will take.

You hold that power within you every day, irrespective of how rich, how clever, how well, how lucky, how trapped, how old or how burdened you are.

There is no greater magic.

From nothing your choices create change. Every precious moment of every day of your existence. Don't have a purpose? Let me give you one.

Your purpose is to lay down at night at peace with yourself and your actions. To know that your choices allowed you to be the best you that you can be without hurting anyone else in the process.

Chapter 11

Keeping It Real

Be Realistic.

Don't fill yourself full of false promises.

No matter how well intentioned. They are going to let you down.

Remember…

> **Education before Choice.**
> **Choice before Action.**
> **Action before Freedom.**

At first glance, change seems hard and scary.

The reality often is it's not change itself but the fear of not knowing the outcome that really scares us.

If you let that fear be the thing that decides whether you become your best, then how does anything get any better?

Be honest with your feelings. At the very least when talking to the person that matters most, namely… yourself.

Cut the bullshit. You deserve this honesty and you'll be surprised what you might uncover that needs help, cheering on, or even applause.

Ask yourself from that honest place…

Am I happy?

What excuses/reasons do I use to stop me going forward?

What do I need?

Are my choices serving me?

What am I chasing?

What's the one thing, if I did it, that would make my day a win?

How can I take one step closer to a good moment or my end aim?

What will **ACTUALLY** work for you when you are stuck?

***

What if the problem is simply that the choices are too many or too hard to choose from?

When choice overwhelms us, the smart thing to do is drop anchor and get advice or education from someone with more knowledge or experience than ourselves. That person may be someone you admire, a professional or further education for yourself.

If you blow the electricity out in your house, you hire an electrician. If your car stops running, you hire a mechanic. Don't you deserve that same level of basic maintenance?

Perhaps an answer to being overwhelmed by choice is to simply limit your choices. Sometimes the sheer number of choices can be immobilising. So you've got to cut some loose – lighten the load. Simplify. **Look at only the very smallest steps forward.**

Or work backwards. Meaning think about your end aim and consider, 'To get to that aim, what do I need to do?' Then make the first step on that path.

Alternatively, try looking at the three most obvious outcomes and make the choice that leads to the one you most want.

If all else fails look for support or help from someone else who has made it past where you are up to. Use someone with life experience in getting past the hurdle that's holding you back.

Small choices matter.

Choosing to read this small book counts as a win as surely as considering its words long after you close its cover. Choosing how to see yourself or your story matters as much or more than what may feel like the big choices of starting a new job, changing careers, choosing what to believe, buying a house, approaching a stranger to form a new relationship or leaving a toxic one. **Start small... small choices matter, from response all the way through to risk, your response to that risk and back again!**

Let me be clear. Putting this line to work in your life means just that: WORK... **On your part.** Particularly because any worthwhile change begins with the hard task of using your own personal bullshit detector. It means searching and stopping the self-sabotage, excuses, reasons, overthinking, people-pleasing, meanness, lies and denial. All of which, speaking from personal experience, is frustrating, frightening, painful and hard to do. The bad news is that you don't just do this once to become who you want to be. You must do it over and over again.

The good news on the bad news.

Every time you are strong enough to do it, it's a tiny bit easier than the time before. It gets easier until it becomes a challenge that feels right and comfortable instead of like hard work. In fact, like anything else, if you do it long enough, it becomes hard not to do.

A quick note on chasing happiness.

This is a hotly debated topic amongst great thinkers of the world. Speaking on behalf of all the people who spent a lot of time chasing it and pulled up empty-handed and feeling pretty ripped off, disappointed and frustrated, I feel it's fair to say the whole happiness thing is a bit of a marketing gig.

Happiness is whatever **you** choose to say it is. For some, it's a moment; for others, a state of mind.

In all reality, it is not so much dancing around, smiling all day but perhaps more the absence of feeling like shit.

Which, once made absent, allows us think better and perhaps smile more often. I am yet to meet anyone out there that, even though they look like they have it all together, doesn't have an unhappy part in their world. To feel unhappy once in a while is normal. To feel good and, once in a while, really happy…also normal.

And if you are the constantly happy kind of human, then well done.

You are, in fact, rare and blessed.

Chapter 12

Who Am I To Direct This Small Book To You?

Why listen to me? I am no one special. I am not a doctor. I have no claim to fame, fortune or success. I have made a great many mistakes in my life and will likely make many more.

What gives me the right to write this small book of thinking to you?

The answer is simple.

Because I am just like you.

I am a human trying to make my best way forward in a world that sometimes doesn't make sense, isn't fair, feels wrong, hurts and doesn't always have answers.

The thing that makes my days worthwhile is showing other people themselves as I see them. It's extraordinary how often people fail to notice their best bits.

But I'll be brutally honest – if this book helps you feel less lonely or gives you a better day today or tomorrow, I wrote it with purely selfish intent! Helping you find your happiness, success, relief, peace, or best self makes me find and be mine.

I would be a fool to write a small book about a specific way of thinking and acting without living my own advice.

So, I made a choice.

My choice was to write this small book.

To you.

And if it helps, even a little bit, then it's been worth sorting through all these thoughts, words, ideas, and beliefs.

Now it's up to you to choose to make yours.

Chapter 13

One Small Thing

You're nearly to the end of this small book.

It is made with the final chapter titled FINAL PAGE.

Should you choose to turn that to that final page, once open, remove it.

Own it. Decorate it, highlight it, copy it, swear at it if it helps. But pin it where you will see it most often.

Make it your focus and do whatever it takes to **keep** it your focus.

REPEAT REPEAT REPEAT

Read the last page out loud.

Throw darts at it if it directs your attention to it.

Then when it's unreadable, rewrite it.

Sing it, dance it, scream it, but most importantly,

<u>LIVE IT.</u>

I can't guarantee life will be better for you.

I can promise you will own a world of your **own** making.

With all this in mind, the final words in this book must be from your mouth.

So should you choose to turn to the final page of this small book, read it **out loud**, with conviction.

<u>Hear your own voice say the words.</u>
<u>Own them.</u>

Say it again and keep saying it till you can hear it and it doesn't sound unnatural to your own ears.

Enjoy. Be brave. And don't fear the judgements of others or yourself.

<u>Fear instead the regret of not being aware your choices!</u>

Chapter 14

FINAL PAGE

TURN AT WILL AND MAY THESE WORDS HELP SHAPE YOUR BEST LIFE

A Small Book

I
HAVE
A
CHOICE

Shawline Publishing Group Pty Ltd
www.shawlinepublishing.com.au

www.ingramcontent.com/pod-product-compliance
Lightning Source LLC
Chambersburg PA
CBHW011959090526
44591CB00018B/2715